EDUFA

Efua T. Sutherland

Afram Publications (Ghana) Ltd.

First Published in 1967
Addison Wesley Longman Group Limited,
Longman House,
Burnt Hill, Harlow,
Essex CM20 2JE,
England

This Edition Published by:
Afram Publications (Ghana) Ltd
P. O. Box M18
Accra, Ghana

Tel: +233 244 314 103/ + 233 554 555 444
Kumasi: +233 554 555 455
Email: sales@aframpubghana.com
            publishing@aframpubghana.com
Website: www.aframpubghana.com

ISBN: 978-9964-70-509-1

Cast

ABENA (*EDUFA'S Sister*)
EDUFA
SEGUWA (*a matronly member of the household*)
AMPOMA (*EDUFA'S wife*)
KANKAM (*EDUFA'S/father*)
CHORUS (*of women from the town*)
SENCHI (*EDUFA'S friend*)
SAM (*an idiot servant*)

Music for the four songs, transcribed by Dr E. Laing, will be found at the end of the text.

The Setting

The courtyard and inner court of Edufa's expensive house. The two areas are linked by wide steps. The inner court is the ground floor of the house. Here, towards the back and slightly off-centre, a slim pillar stands from floor to ceiling. Behind this pillar is a back wall. There are also two flanking walls, left and right. Short flights of steps between back and side walls lead into Edufa's rooms on the left, and guest rooms on the right. A door in the right wall, close to the courtyard steps, leads into the kitchen. There are three long, box-like seats, which match the colour of the pillar. Two of these are close to the courtyard steps, against the side walls; one is right of the pillar.

An atmosphere of elegant spaciousness is dominant.

For Act Three, the seats are shifted to more convenient positions, and light garden chairs, a trestle table and a drinks trolley are moved in.

People in the audience are seated in Edufa's courtyard. The gate by which they have entered is the same one the chorus and other characters use as directed in the play.

[*ABENA is sitting on side seat, her head resting on her knees, her cloth wrapped round her for warmth. She is gazing into a small, black, water pot which stands on the step below her. Another pot, red, stands on the floor beside her. She tilts the black pot, measuring its contents with her eyes. Then she looks up, sighs wearily and rubs her eyes as if she can no longer keep sleep away.*]

ABENA: [*Beginning slowly and sleepily*]
                Night is long when our eyes are unsleeping.
                Three nights long my eyes have been unsleeping,
                Keeping wakeful watch on the dew falling,
                Falling from the eaves...

                [*She glances anxiously round the inner court, rises, goes towards the steps leading to EDUFA's rooms, hesitates and turns back.*]

                And dreaming.
                Dreamlike views of mist rising
                Above too much water everywhere. I heard tonight,
                A voice stretched thin through the mist, calling.
                Heard in that calling, the quiver of Ampoma's voice.
                Thought I saw suddenly in the restless white waters,
                The laterite red of an ant-hill-jutting
                And rocking.
                A misty figure on its topmost tip,
                Flicking her fingers like one despairing.

I panicked, and came to this door, listening,
But all was silence —
Night is so deceiving when our eyes
Are robbed too long of sleep.

[*She returns to her seat, puts her head back on her knees and is soon singing.*]

O, child of Ama,
Child of Ama in the night
Is wandering,
Crying, 'Mm-m-m-m,
How my mother is pondering.'
O, child of Ama,
Why is she wandering,
     Why wandering,
Why wand'ring in the night
Like the dying?
Mewuo!

[*She keeps up the last bars of the song for a while, patting the black pot with one hand, and her own arm with the other in a manner suggestive of self-consolation. Presently, she looks into the sky again.*]

But my last night of wakefulness is over.

[*She rises, tipping the black pot.*]

The last drop of dew has fallen. There's enough dew water in the pot. [*She picks up the pot, and tilts the red one.*] And here is stream water from the very eye of the spring where the red rock weeps without ceasing. [*Gesturing towards EDUFA'S rooms*] My brother Edufa, your orders are done, though I obey without understanding ... [*Walking about*]

Here in this house, where there was always someone laughing, suddenly no one feels like smiling. I've never known such silence in my brother's house. Mm? It is unnatural. From rising until sleep claimed us again at night, people came through our gate; for who doesn't know my brother Edufa in this town? Benevolent one, who doesn't love him? Old and young, they came. They brought laughter. Those who brought sadness returned with smiles, comforted.

Why then does brother shut our gate to stop such flow of friends? Mm? True that Ampoma, his wife, is unwell; but if she is unwell, should we not open our gate? She is not mortally ill; but even so, just let it be known, and sympathy and comforting gifts would flow in from every home. So much does the whole town hold her dear. [*Yawning*] Oh well ... I don't even know what it is that ails her. Their door is barred, and my brother says nothing to me. [*Yawning again*] Ha! Tired. [*She picks up the red pot also, carrying the two pressed against her body.*] Well ... I place these at his door ... [*She places them at the top of the steps.*] ... and make my way ... to ... [*Yawning*] sleep. I don't know why I should be so sad. [*She crosses, humming her song, and goes out through the kitchen door.*]

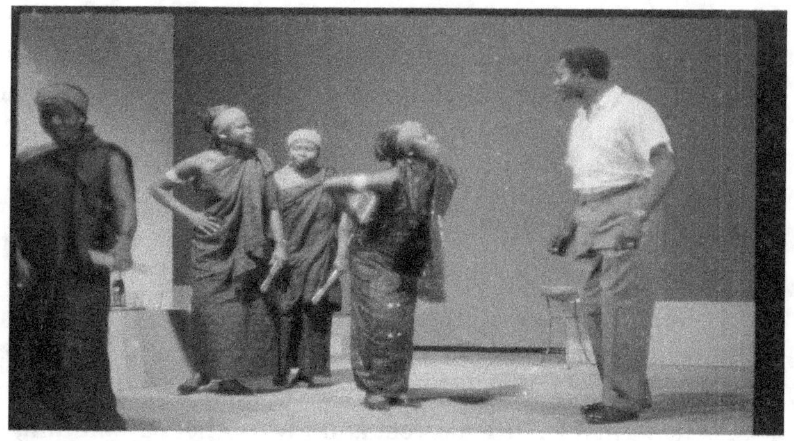

Scene One

[Edufa's hands reach out and pick up the pots. He is heard issuing instructions urgently to someone inside]

Edufa: Pour first the dew water, and then the stream water, over the herbs in the bathroom. Quickly. Then bring out fire for the incense.

          [Outside the courtyard walls, a chorus of women is heard performing]

Chorus: *[Chanting to the rhythm of wooden clappers]*
          Our mother's dead
          Ei! Ei! — Ei!
          We the orphans cry,
          Our mother's dead,
          O! O — O!
          We the orphans cry.

          [The chanting repeats. As the voices, the clack-clack accompaniment and the thudding of running feet recede, Seguwa comes hurriedly out of Edufa's rooms. She listens as she crosses to the kitchen, and is clearly disturbed by the performance. Her brief absence from the court is filled in by the chanting which becomes dominant once again as the chorus return past the house. She comes back, carrying a brazier in which charcoal fire is burning in a small earthen pot. She hesitates by the kitchen door, still preoccupied with the performance outside. At the same time Edufa rushes out in pajamas and dressing gown. He carries a box of incense, and has the air of a man under considerable mental strain]

Edufa: Why are they doing a funeral chant? They are not coming towards this house? [*To Seguwa*] You've spoken to no one?

Seguwa: [*With some resentment*] To no one. My tongue is silenced. [*Pause*] It must be for someone else's soul they clamour. [*The chanting fades*]

Edufa: [*Composing himself*] No, they are not coming here. [*Pause*] Put the fire down.

[*Seguwa places the fire closes to the central seat. Edufa rips the box open, and flings incense nervously on the fire*]

Keep the incense burning while Ampoma and I bathe in the herbs.

Seguwa: It seems to me that the time has come now to seek some other help. All this bathing in herbs and incense burning; I don't see it bringing much relief to your wife Ampoma in there.

Edufa: Doubting?

Seguwa: I'm not saying I doubt anything. You have chosen me to share this present burden with you, and I'm letting my mouth speak so that my mind can have some ease. It is I myself who say I'm hardy, but how can I help having a woman's bowels?

Edufa: Calm yourself. I cannot give in to any thoughts of hopelessness. Where is your faith? I thought I could trust it.

Seguwa: You can trust my secrecy; that I have sworn; though what I have sworn to keep secret now frets against the closed walls of my skull. I haven't sworn to have faith against all reason. No, not in the face of your wife's condition in that bedroom there. Let's call for help.

Edufa: [*With indications of despair*] From whom? We are doing everything we can. Also, it is Ampoma's wish that no one should be allowed to see her.

Seguwa: And is she dead that we should be bound to honour her wishes? She is not herself. In her present state we can expect her to say childish things. The sick are like children. Let me call for help.

It is almost unnatural that even the mother who bore her should be kept ignorant of her sickness, serious as it now is. Ah, poor mother; if we could but see her now. She is probably pampering the children you've sent to her, keeping them happy, and thinking she is relieving her daughter for rest and fun with you, her husband. [*Bitterly*] How you are deceived, mother.

Edufa: Don't fret so much. Calm yourself, will you?

Seguwa: It is your wife who needs calming, if I may say so.

Edufa: You've promised to stand with me in this trouble. You will, won't you? Your service and your courage these last few days have given me strength and consolation. Don't despair now. Ampoma is getting better.

Seguwa: Better? Ho, ho. After fainting twice last night? [*Shrugs*] Ah, well, just as you say. I promised to stand with you and will. But may God help us all, for the bridge we are now crossing is between the banks of life and the banks of death. And I do not know which way we're facing. [*Pause*] Where is the incense? I'll keep it burning.

Edufa: [*Relieved*] Your kindness will not be forgotten, believe me, when we can smile again in this house. [*He gives her the box. She sprinkles more incense on the fire*] See that the gate is barred

Scene Two

[Ampoma has appeared unnoticed at the top of the steps, and is standing there unsteadily. There is a look of near insanity about her. Seguwa sees her first, and lets out a stifled scream]

Edufa: *[Hurrying to her]* Oh, Ampoma. You shouldn't leave your bed. You shouldn't come out here.

Ampoma: *[Weakly]* The sun is shining on the world, and I am… falling. *[She totters]*

Seguwa: Hold her! She'll fall.

Edufa: *[Only just saving Ampoma from falling]* Is the gate barred?

Seguwa: *[With uncontrolled irritation]* O, God! I cannot understand it. *[She picks up a wrap Ampoma has dropped on the steps, starts towards the gate, but gives up in confusion and returns to the incense burning]*

Ampoma: *[Moving and compelling Edufa who is supporting her, to move with her]* I have come out into the bright sun. There is no warmth in my bed. And no comfort. Only darkness.

Edufa: Sit, then, Let us sit together here. *[He urges her tenderly to the seat near the kitchen door, takes the wrap from Seguwa and arranges it round her shoulders]*
You want to be in the sun? That means you are getting well. You are. Tell yourself you are. Make your soul will your strength back again. *[Pause]* In a little while we will bathe in the herbs, and later today, at the junction between day and night, we will bathe again, the final time. Tomorrow… tomorrow, you will feel much better. I promise you.

Ampoma: *[Dreamily]* Tomorrow? When… is tomorrow?
[She droops, and quickly buries her face in the nape of Edufa's neck]

Edufa: [*Confused*] Tomorrow…

Ampoma: [*Breaking free*] Oh, no! I cannot have them straying.

[*Seguwa picks up the wrap she flings away, and hover anxiously in the background*]

Edufa: [*Helplessly*] What? Who?

Ampoma: Like two little goats. I'm leaving them. I? Two little goats struggling on the far away hillside. I see their eyes glowing in the dark; lonely. Oh, my little boy! And you, my girl with breasts just budding! What hands will prepare you for your wedding? [*She sobs quietly*]

Seguwa: She is talking of her children. Thank God they are not here to see this sight.

Edufa: [*To Ampoma*] Don't talk as if all were ending. All is not ending. It cannot end. [*To Seguwa*] Put on more incense. [*He guides Ampoma back to the seat*]

Ampoma: [*On the way*] My bed is so full of a river of my own tears, I was drowning there. [*Helplessly*] Why do we weep so much?
             [*They sit*]

Edufa: Dreams. You only dreamed these things. Sickness plagues the mind with monstrous fantasies. Pay no heed to them. Think only of reality… Think of me. Is not your bed that sunny place in which we plant our children? There has never been anything but warmth and happiness there and never will be, as long as I live and love you so.

Ampoma: Don't speak of it. I have strayed into the cold. Yet, how good that I should not be the one to live beyond your days. I could not live where you are not. I could not live without you, my husband.

Edufa: Ah, loving wife.

Ampoma: Yes, That is the truth. I have loved you.

Edufa: You have. And I have you still to fill my days with joy. [*He puts his arm round her protectively*]

Ampoma: [*Looking sadly at him*] I am dying too young, don't you think? Look at me. [*She rises abruptly*] What am I saying? We knew this day could come. Am I listening to the lure of his voice at this final stage? Weakening at the closeness of his flesh? [*To Edufa*] Help me. Take your arm away from me. Why do you restrain me at your peril?

Edufa: Come inside. You've been out there too long already.

Ampoma: [*More calmly, moving again, halting now and then*] Let me talk with you a little longer in the sun before I step into the dark where you cannot see me. Soon, my pledge will be honoured. I am leaving our children motherless in your hands. Let me hear you say you love them, though I know you do.

Edufa: I love them, Ampoma.

Ampoma: And will you keep them from harm? Protect them?

Edufa: How else would I be worthy of the sacred name of father? How worthy of your trust, brave woman? No harm shall come to the children that I can prevent.

Ampoma: I fear the harm that might come to them from another woman's dissatisfied heart.

Edufa: Ampoma, what are you saying? Another woman? I swear that in this, as in nothing else, true triumph is mine. You inspire devotion, incomparable one. There is no other woman beside you.

Ampoma: The dead are removed. Time must, and will soften pain for the living. If you should marry another woman, will she not envy my children, because you have them with your own love and mine combined?

Edufa: Poor Ampoma. In what unfamiliar world is your mind wandering that you speak so strangely?

Ampoma: Promise me that you will never place them in another woman's power. Never risk their lives in the hands of

	another. Promise me that, and I will die without that unbearable fear here in my heart.
Edufa:	You will not die. But if it will calm you to hear it, I do promise.
Ampoma:	That you will not marry again?
Edufa:	That no other woman will cross my inner door, nor share my bed. This house will never even harbour a woman not of my own blood, at whom my eye could look without restraint.
Ampoma:	Swear it.
Edufa:	I swear it.
Ampoma:	[*Calmly walking away from him*] Over me, the sun is getting dark. [*With great agitation*] My husband! Watch the death that you should have died. [*She frets from place to place as if escaping from him*] Stay over there in the sun. Children! My children! If I could cross this water, I would pluck you back from the mountain side. Children! Hold my hand! [*She stretches out her hand to the vision that she alone can see*]
Edufa:	[*Catching hold of her*] Oh, wife of my soul. You should never have made that fatal promise.
Ampoma:	That I loved you? My love has killed me. [*Faintness comes over her. She falls into Edufa's arms*] Children! And... mother ...mother. [*Edufa takes her in, almost carrying her. Seguwa, not quite knowing how to help, follows them*]
Chorus:	[*Heard again in the distance*] Our mother's dead, Ei, Ei, — Ei! We the orphans cry, Our mother's dead, O! O — O! We the orphans cry. [*The voices travel further into the distance*]

Scene Three

Seguwa:

[*Returning*] This is what we are living with. This weakness that comes over her, and all this meandering talk. Talk of water and of drowning? What calamitous talk is that? When will it end?

How will it end? We are mystified. How wouldn't we be? Oh, we should ask Edufa some questions; that is what I say. You should all ask Edufa some questions.

[*She goes to the fire, throws in more incense, and withdraws from it as if she hates it*]

I wish I could break this lock on my lips. Let those who would gamble with lives,
Stake their own.
None I know of flesh and blood,
Has right to stake another's life
For his own.
Edufa! You have done Ampoma wrong,
And wronged her mother's womb.
Ah, Mother! Mother!
The scenes I have witnessed in here,
In this respected house,
Would make torment in your womb.
Your daughter, all heart for the man
She married, keeps her agonies from you.
Ah, mother! Mother!
Edufa has done Ampoma wrong.
Tafrakye!
Some matters weight down the tongue, But mother, I swear
Edufa does Ampoma wrong,
He does her wrong.

[*She returns angrily to the incense burning*]

Scene Four

[Kankam enters through the gate. Hearing his footsteps. Seguwa turns round in alarm. She is torn between surprise and fear when she notices who has arrived. Kankam stops on the courtyard steps]

Seguwa: *[Approaching him hesitantly]* Grandfather!

Kankam: *[Quietly]* Yes. It is me. Three years, is it? Three years since I walked out of that same gate, a disappointed father. Three years. Well… tell him I am here.

Seguwa: Tell Edufa?

Kankam: Yes, the man whom nature makes my son.

Seguwa: Oh, grandfather, do I dare? So troubled is his mood, he has ordered his gate shut against all callers.

Kankam: *[With power]* Call him.

Seguwa: *[Nervously]* As for me, I'm willing enough to call him, but…

Kankam: *[An angry tap of his umbrella emphasising his temper]* Call him! It was I who bore him.

Seguwa: *[On her knees, straining to confide]* Oh, grandfather, help him, help him. God sent you here, I'm sure. I could tell you things… no, I couldn't tell you. Oh, please forget your quarrel with him and help us all. What shall I say? Hmm. His wife Ampoma is sick, very sick.

Kankam: So, he bars his door; just in case anyone looks in to offer help… *[Calling with authority]* Edufa! Edufa!

Seguwa: *[Hurrying]* I will call him. He was bathing. [She meets Edufa coming out of his rooms]

Edufa: *[Seeing his father and recoiling]* You? What do you want? *[His eyes shift uneasily as Kankam stares hard at him. He comes down the steps]* What do you want? Three years ago, you declared me not fit to be your son and left my house. Had my position not been well evaluated in this town, you might have turned

	tongues against me as the man who drove his own father out of his home. What do you want now?
Kankam:	[*Walking deliberately to the seat near the kitchen*] Yes. It has burnt down to loveless greetings between father and son, I know. What do I want? I will tell you presently. [*He sits*] Don't let us fail, however, on the sacredness of courtesy. Had I entered the house of a total stranger, he would have given me water to drink, seeing I'm a traveller.

[*Edufa is embarrassed, but at that moment Seguwa is already bringing water from the kitchen*]

I happen to be your father, and you a man in whose house, water is the least of the things that overflow. [*Seguwa gives the water to Kankam, who pours a little on the floor Stylistically for libation, drinks it, and thanks her. She returns to the kitchen*]

Edufa:	[*Awkwardly*] Well?
Kankam:	Sit down, son, Sit.

[*Edufa sits uneasily on the opposite seat*]

What do I want, you say? [*Very deliberately*] I want the courage that makes responsible men. I want truthfulness. Decency. Feeling for your fellow men. These are the things I've always wanted. Have you got them to give?

[*Edufa rises, angry*]

I fear not, since you have sold such treasures to buy yourself the importance that fools admire.

Edufa:	If you have come only to tempt me to anger, then leave my house.

Kankam:	Oh, stop blabbering. I left before, and will do so again, but it isn't any absurd rage that will drive me out.
Edufa:	What do you want, I say?
Kankam:	[*With terrible self control*] The life of your wife Ampoma, from you.
Edufa:	[*Very nervous*] And you mean by that?

[*Kankam only stares at him*]

	What makes me keeper of her life?
Kankam:	Marriage, and her innocent love. [*A chilly pause*] Oh, I know it all, Edufa. You cannot hide behind impudence and lies; not with me. Diviners are there for all of us to consult. [*Edufa winces*] And deeds done in secret can, by the same process, be brought to light.
Edufa:	You know nothing. Diviners! Ho! Diviners? What have Diviners got to do with me?
Kankam:	That, you must tell me. I believe in their ancient art. I know, at least, that Ampoma is sick, and could die. It has been revealed to me that she could die. And why? That you might live.
Edufa:	Absurd. It is not true…Ampoma is a little ill, that's all. She has fever… that's all… Yes… that's all. You are deceived.
Kankam:	Deceived. That I am. Am I not? Look at me and tell me it is not true. [*Edufa's eyes shift nervously*] He cannot. How could he? [*Pauses*] I went to my own diviner to consult him about my health. He spread his holy patch of sand, lit candles, and over his sacred bowl of water, made incantation; and scrawled his mystic symbols in the sand.
	I'll tell you what he saw in his divination, for it was all about you, my son. [*Advancing on Edufa*] four years ago, you went to consult one such diviners.

Edufa: Do you want me to take you seriously? You cannot believe all this, you who educated me to lift me to another plane of living.

Kankam: That's all right, my man. Most of us consult diviners for our protection. All men need to feel secure in their inmost hearts.

Edufa: I am not all men. I am emancipated.

Kankam: As emancipated as I'll show. Your diviners saw death hanging over your life — a normal mortal condition, I would think. But what happened, coward, what happened, when he said you could avert the danger by the sacrifice of another life?

Edufa: He lies.

Kankam: Who? Has that not been heard before? Has that not been said to many of us mortal men? Why were you not content, like all of us, to purge your soul by offering gifts of cola and white calico to the needy, and sacrificing a chicken or a sheep, or, since you can afford it, a cow?

Edufa: Are you all right, father?

Kankam: Beasts are normal sacrifices, but surely, you know they are without speech. Beasts swear no oaths to die for others, Edufa. [*Pause*] Were you not afraid, being husband and father, that someone dear to your blood, might be the one to make the fatal oath over that powerful charm you demanded, and become its victim?

Edufa: This is intolerable. I will hear no more. [*He makes for his rooms*]

Kankam: [*With quiet menace, barring his way*] You will hear it all, unless you'd rather have me broadcast my story in the marketplace, and turn you over to the judgement of the town.

[*Edufa stops, sensitive to the threat*]

	My diviner does not lie. The very day itself when all this happened was clearly engraved in sand.
Edufa:	[*Huffily*] All right, all-seeing, prove it. [*He sits*]
Kankam:	[*Standing over him*] It had been raining without relief since the night before. Dampness had entered our very bones, and no one's spirits were bright. But you were of all of us, most moody and morose; in fact, so fractious that you snapped at your wife for merely teasing that you couldn't bear, for once, to be shut away from your precious business and society. It was as if you couldn't tolerate yourself, or us. Suddenly you jumped up and rushed out into the raging storm. That was the day you did your evil and killed your wife.
Edufa:	Great God! If you were not my father, I would call you…
Kankam:	Towards evening you returned. The rain had stopped, and we of the household were sitting here, in this very place to catch what warmth there was in the sickly sunset. You seemed brighter then, for which change we all expressed our thankfulness. In fact, contrarily, you were cheerful, though still a little restless. How could we have known you were carrying on you the hateful charm? How could we have suspected it, when your children were playing round you with joyful cries? How could we have known it was not a joke, when you suddenly leaned back and asked which of us loved you well enough to die for you, throwing the question into the air with studied carelessness? Emancipated one, how could we have known of your treachery?
Edufa:	[*Rising*] incredible drivel! Incredible. Is this the man I have loved as father?
Kankam:	You had willed that some old wheezier like me should be the victim. And I was the first to speak.

"Not me, my son," said I am joking. "Die your own death. I have mine to die." And we all laughed. Do you remember? My age was protecting me. [*Pause*] Then Ampoma spoke. [*Pause*] Yes, I see you wince in the same manner as you did when she spoke the fatal words that day and condemned her life. 'I will die for you Edufa', she said; and meant it too, poor, doting woman.

Edufa: Father, are you mad?

Kankam: [*Shocked*] Nyame above! To say father and call me mad! My ntoro within you shivers with the shock of it!

Edufa: [*Aware that he has violated taboo*] You provoked me.

Kankam: [*Moving away*] All right, stranger, I am mad! And madness is uncanny. Have you not noticed how many a time the mad seem to know things hidden from men in their right minds? [*Rounding up on Edufa*] You know you killed your wife that day. I saw fear in your eyes when she spoke. I saw it, but I didn't understand.

I have learned that in your chamber that night, you tried to make her forswear the oath she had innocently sworn. But the more you pleaded, the more emotionally she swore away her life for love of you; until, driven by your secret fear, you had to make plain to her the danger in which she stood. You showed her the charm. You confessed to her its power to kill whoever swore to die for you. Don't you remember how she wept? She had spoken and made herself the victim. Ampoma has lived with that danger ever since, in spite of all your extravagant efforts to counter the potency of the charm by washings and rites of purification. [*With great concern*] Edufa, I am here because I fear that time has come to claim that vow.

Edufa:	Leave me alone, will you? [*He sits miserably*]
Kankam:	Confess it or deny it.
Edufa:	I owe you no such duty. Why don't you leave me alone?
Kankam:	To kill? Say to myself, 'Father, your son wants to murder', and go? All the world's real fathers would not wish a murderer for a son, my son. Yes, in spite of my rage there is still truth of father and son between us.
Edufa:	Rest. My wife, Ampoma, is not dying.
Kankam:	If she does not die it will be by the intervention of some great power alone. An oath once sworn will always ride its swearer. But there might still be a chance to save her.
Edufa:	Indeed, in this age, there are doctors with skill enough to sell for what's ailing her, and I can pay their fees.
Kankam:	[*Pleading*] Confess and denounce your wrong. Bring out that evil charm. And before Ampoma and all of us, whose souls are corporate in this household, denounce it. Burn it. The charm may not be irrevocably done if we raise the prayer of our souls together.
Edufa:	Will it help you if I swear that there is no ground for all your worry? And now will you let me go?
Kankam:	[*With anguish*] Hush! You swear? Oh, my son, I have finished. I can do no more. Have you sunk so low in cowardice? If you must lie, don't swear about it in a house in which death is skirmishing, and the ancestral spirits stand expectantly by. A man may curse himself from his own lips. Do not curse the house in which your children have to grow.
	Spirits around us, why don't you help him save himself. When he went to consult the diviner, he was already doing well. You could tell. If you looked at his new clothes you could tell. If you looked at his well-

appointed house in whose precincts hunger wouldn't dwell.

Already, the town's pavements knew when it was, he who was coming. Nudging announced him. Eyes pivoted to catch his smile. [*With disgust*] You could see all the ivory teeth and all the slimy way down the glowing gullets of those who were learning to call him sir. For he was doing well in the art of buying friends by street benevolence.

Edufa: [*Seizing on a diversion*] Now you betray yourself. It has taken me all these years to probes the core of your antagonism. From what you say, it is clear at last that you envied me. Oh! What lengths a man will go to hide his envy?

Kankam: Pitiful.

Edufa: Fathers are supposed to share with pride in their sons' good fortune. I was not so blessed. My father envied me and turned enemy — even while he ate the meat and salt of my good fortune.

Kankam: Pitiful.

Edufa: And there was I, thinking that enemies could only be encountered outside my gates.

Kankam: Pitiful. At my age, a man has learned to aim his envy at the stars. [*Suffering*] Pity him, you spirits. He grew greedy and insensitive; insane for gain; frantic for the fluff of flattery. And I cautioned him. Did I not warn him? I tried to make him step at the point when we men must be content or let ourselves be lured on to our doom. But he wouldn't listen. He doesn't listen. It makes me ill. Violently ill. I vomit the meat and salt I ate out of ignorance from his hand.

I have finished. [*Pause*] It wouldn't be too much to ask to see the lady before I leave?

Edufa: She mustn't be disturbed.

Kankam: [*Picking up his umbrella from the seat*] Well… as you wish, noble husband. There are enough women, I suppose, ready to fall for your glamour and line up to die for you. I am leaving. Forever now. [*He steps into the courtyard*]

Edufa: One moment.

[*Kankam turns to him hopefully*]

I hope you haven't talked like this to anyone.
You could do so much harm. Unjustly.

Kankam: [*With a rage of disappointment*] Worm. Coward. You are afraid for your overblown reputation, aren't you? You are afraid that if the town got to know they would topple you. No. I am tied by my fatherhood, even though I am not proud that my life water animated you. I'll let them bow to a worm. In time they are bound to know they're bowing too low for their comfort. Were this matter a simple case of crime, I would perhaps seek solution by bringing you to secular justice. As it is, to try still to save the woman's life; our remedy is more probable in the paths of prayer, which I now go to pursue away from your unhelpful presence. [*He leaves*]

Edufa: Alone.
Tears within me that I haven't had the privilege to shed. Father! Call him back that I may weep on his shoulder.

Why am I afraid of him? He would stand with me, even though he rages so.

Call him back to bear me on the strength of his faith.

He knows it all. I can swear he is too true a man to play me foul. But I could not risk confirming it. I dread the power by which he knows, and it shall not gain admission here to energies that which all is set this day to exercise.

Don't ask me why I did it; I do not know the answer. If I must be condemned, let me not be charged for any will to kill, but for my failure to create a faith.

Who thought the charm made any sense? Not I. A mystic symbol by which to calm my fears — that was all I could concede it.

It still doesn't make any sense. And yet, how it frets me, until I'm a leaf blown frantic in a whirlwind.

If only I hadn't been so cynical. I bent my knee where I have no creed and I'm constrained for my mockery.

Hush, oh voice of innocence! Still you're whining in the wind. Unsay it. Do not swear for I am compromised.

She who lies there must recover if ever I'm to come to rest. I love my wife, I love her. My confidence is her hope and her faith in me, mine.

So, are we locked.

Scene One

[The Chorus is heard approaching Edufa's house]

Chorus: Ei! Ei! — Ei!
               We the orphans cry,
               Our mother's dead
               O! O — O!
               We the orphans cry.

               *[They enter through the gate at a run. Their exuberance
               and gaiety would belie the solemn nature of their ritual
               observance. They stop below the courtyard steps]*

Chorus One: *[Calling]* May we enter? Are there no people in this
               beautiful house?
Chorus Two: In the house of the open gate?
Chorus Three: In the house of He-Whose-Hands-Are-Ever-Open?
Chorus: Open Face
               Open Heart
               Open Palm,
               Edufa.
Chorus Four: Come; scratch our palms with a golden coin.
Chorus Five: With a golden nugget.
Chorus: For luck and good fortune.

Chorus One: *[Stepping up]* And Ampoma the beautiful; where is
               she? Woman of this house of fortune. Singing your
               husband's praise is singing your praises too. Tender
               heart who nurses him to his fortune. Stand side by
               side while we beat envious evil out of your house.
Chorus: Are there no people in this beautiful house?
Seguwa: *[Entering from the kitchen]* Who let you in…?
Chorus: *[Cheerfully]* The gate of this house is always open.
Seguwa: *[Uneasily]* Well… greeting…

Chorus:	We answer you.
Seguwa:	[*Still hesitating at the kitchen door*] And you have come…?
Chorus One:	We have come to drive evil away, is the man of the house in? And the lady? We are driving evil out of town.
Chorus:	From every home From street and lane From every corner of our town. Ei! Ei! — Ei! We the orphans cry.
Chorus:	[*Steps up, sniffing and trying to locate the scent*] Incense.
Seguwa:	[*Moving quickly forward*] Whose funeral sends you out in ceremony?
Chorus:	Another's, and our own. It's all the same. While we mourn another's death, it's our own death we also mourn.
Seguwa:	[*Touched*] True. [*She wipes away a tear*]
Chorus:	[*Crowding near her*] Oh, don't let us sadden you.
Seguwa:	There is so much truth in what you say. I would say, do your rite and go in peace for it is most necessary here. I would say, do your rite and do it most religiously, for it is necessary here. I would say it, but I am not owner of this house.
Chorus One:	Why do you hesitate? Is Edufa not in?
Seguwa:	I am trying to make up my mind whether he should be in or out.
Chorus Two:	Well, if a man is in, he's in; and if he is out, he's out. Which is it?
Chorus One:	Make up your mind, for soon, noon will be handing over its power to the indulgent afternoon, and our ritual is timed with the rigours of high noon. Which is it? Is he in or out?
Seguwa:	For driving evil out, he is in, I suppose.

Chorus:	Aha! Then call him.
Seguwa:	I will do my best to bring him out.
Chorus Two:	Do your best?
Seguwa:	Well… I mean … Ampoma, his wife, is lying down… and…
Chorus One:	And it is heard for him to tear himself away… Aha!
Seguwa:	Yes…No…Well… lets me go and find out. I can make up my mind better away from your questioning eyes. [*With a gesture of invitation as she makes for Edufa's rooms*] Wait.
Chorus:	We are waiting. [*They surge into the court*]
Chorus One:	What's her trouble? There was a riot in her eyes.
Chorus Two:	We haven't come to beat her. [*Showing her clappers*] These aren't cudgels to chastise our fellow men. These are for smacking the spirits of calamity.
Chorus One:	[*Snidely*] Ampoma is lying down, she said.
Chorus Two:	[*Laughing*] sick, or lying down in the natural way?
Chorus Three:	I would say, simply rich. Would you not do the same in her place? Let her enjoy her ease.
Chorus Four:	Imagine the fun of it. [*She goes to the seat, right, and mimes lying down luxuriously, much to the enjoyment of her friends*] O lady, lady lying in a bed of silk! What kind of thighs, what kind of thighs must a woman have to earn a bed of silk? A bed of silk, O! If I had her life to live, I wouldn't be out of bed at eleven o'clock in the morning either. Never, O!

[*In the middle of this fun making, Edufa rushes out. He stops short at the sight. But the mood of hilarity there compels him to a show of humour*]

Chorus:	[*Running up to crowd round him*] Husband!
Chorus One:	Aha! The giver himself.
Chorus:	Greeting.
Edufa:	I answer. Well? … Well?

Chorus One: We would not dream of passing up your house while we do our rite.

Edufa: Whose death is it? Is the rite for a new funeral?

Chorus One: No. It's for an old sorrow out of which time has dried the tears. You can say that we are doing what gives calamity and woe the final push in the back — which is a manner of speaking only, as you know…

Edufa: And you have come here…

Chorus One: To purge your house also in the same old manner, for calamity is for all mankind and none is free from woe.

Edufa: Thank you. You may proceed.

Chorus Two: [*In fun*] Then cross our palms with the gleam of luck. And gives us a welcome drink.

              [*Edufa motions to Seguwa who goes to the kitchen to get drinks, taking the brazier away with her*]

              And let the beautiful one, your wife, know that we are here.

Edufa: She is not very well today.

Chorus: [*Genuinely*] Oh! Sorry.

Edufa: Nothing serious. In fact, she is getting better.

Chorus: [*Relaxing*] Good. We greet her and wish her well.

Edufa: She thanks you. Welcome in her name and from myself as well. [*He takes a big gold ring off his finger and touches the palm of each of the women with it saying*]
              Good luck and good fortune to you, friends.

              [*Seguwa brings drinks on a tray which she places on the seat near the kitchen*]

              And here are your drinks.

Chorus One: [*Solemnly*] Come, friends. Let's do the ceremony for the benevolent one.

Chorus: [*Becoming formal*] Evil has no place here. Nor
                 anywhere. Away, away.

                 [*Moving rhythmically at a slow running pace through
                 the court and courtyard, they perform their ritual with
                 solemnity*]

                 [*Chanting*] Our mother's dead,
                 Ei! Ei! — Ei!
                 We the orphans cry,
                 O! O — O!
                 We the orphans cry.

                 [*Speaking at a halt*]

                 Crying the death day of another is carrying your own
                 death day. While we mourn for another, we mourn
                 for ourselves. One's death is the death of all mankind.
                 Comfort! Comfort to us all,
                 Comfort!
                 Away evil, away.
                 Away all calamity,
                 Away!

                 [*Chanting on the move*]

                 Our mother's dead,
                 Ei! Ei! — Ei!
                 We the orphans cry,
                 Our mother's dead,
                 O! O — O!
                 We the orphan's cry.

                 [*During this ritual Seguwa stands attentively in the
                 background. Edufa remains just above the courtyard
                 steps, intensely quiet, eyes shut in private prayer. The
                 chorus finishes up on the steps below, facing him*]

Chorus One: There now. We have done. Health to you. [*Edufa is too removed to hear her*] Health to you, Edufa, and to your wife and all your household. [*To her companions*] See how he is moved. We have done right to come to the house of one as pious as he.

Chorus Two: Such faith must surely bring him blessing.

Edufa: [*Stirring*] Your drinks await you.
                [*The mood of the chorus changes to light-heartedness again*]

Chorus One: [*As her companions collect their drinks, her own glass in hand*] That's right. Tears and laughter. That's how it is. It isn't all tears and sorrow, my friends. Tears and laughter. It isn't all want and pain. With one hand we wipe away the unsweet water. And with the other we raise a cup of sweetness to our lips. It isn't all tears, my friends, this world of humankind.

Chorus: [*Drinks in hand*] May you be blessed, Edufa.

Edufa: [hurrying them up nicely] Drink up. Day is piling up its hours, and you must be eager to attend the business of your own homes. It was good of you to come. [*He contrives to draw Seguwa aside*] Go in there. Ampoma was sleeping. It would not do for her to walk out into this. [*Seguwa hurries into Edufa's rooms*] You did well to come. A man needs friendship. But it's late in the morning, and you are women…with homes to feed.

Chorus One: We will come again to greet your wife.

Edufa: [*Skillfully herding them out*] Yes, yes…

Chorus Two: Would you sit us at your generous table? Eat with us?

Chorus Three: Charm us?

Edufa: Yes, All is good time… some day soon.

Seguwa: [*Running out happily*] Edufa! Edufa! She has asked for food.

Edufa: [*Excitedly*] for food. She has?

Seguwa: [*Making fast for the kitchen*] for soup. She says, I would like some fresh fish soup. Thank God.

Edufa:	Thank God. Get it.
Seguwa:	After three days without interest…
Edufa:	Get it quickly.
Seguwa:	Thank God. [*She enters the kitchen*]
Edufa:	[*Calling after her*] Is there fish in the house? If not, send out instantly. Thank God. [*Stretching out his hands to the chorus*] Victory, my friends.
Chorus One:	[*Puzzled*] So relieved. Ampoma must be more ill than he cared to let us know. Thank God.
Chorus Two:	He is wise not to spill the troubles of his house in public.
Edufa:	[*On his way in*] Thank you friends. I must leave you now.

Scene Two

[*As Edufa and the Chorus are leaving, Senchi, carrying a small, battered leather case, swings in flamboyantly, whistling to announce himself*]

Senchi: … and the wanderer… the wanderer… the wanderer comes home. [Seeing the Chorus] comes in the nick of time when everything he loves is together in one place. Friends, women, bottles… [*His laughter is all pervasive*]

Edufa: [*Thrilled*] Senchi!

Senchi: [*Airily to the chorus*] Good afternoon. My name is Senchi, and I'm always lucky. I love women, and always find myself right in the middle of them. Welcome me.

Chorus Four: [*Quite pleased*] He's quite a fellow.

Senchi: She's right.

Edufa: Senchi. What brings you here?

Senchi: [*Stepping up to him*] Life… brings me here. Welcome me.

Edufa: Indeed. You've come in excellent time.

Senchi: And what are you doing here? Practicing polygamy? Or big-mammy? Or what? Anyone you choose to declare will be against the law. I'm in transit, as usual. May I spend the night with you?

Edufa: But certainly. Do me the favour. It's very good to see you, and my privilege to house one as lucky as you obviously are.

Senchi: [*To chorus*] Now he flatters.

Edufa: I only wish we were better prepared to receive you.

Senchi: Impossible [his eyes on the chorus] You couldn't improve on this welcome here. All good stock, by their looks. Local breed? They're not dressed for fun and games, though, are they? Pity.

Chorus Three: [*Approvingly*] He's quite a fellow.

Senchi: [*Sniffing*] and I smell — what is that I smell? Incense? [*To Edufa*] Say, have you changed your religion again? What are you practicing now? Catholicism, spiritualism, neo-theosophy or what? Last time I passed through here, you were an intellectual atheist, or something in that category. I wouldn't be surprised to see you turned Buddhist monk next time. [*The chorus are leaving*] Don't go when I've only just come. [*To Edufa*] What are they going away for?

Chorus: Our work is finished here.

Edufa: They've been doing a ceremony here. Don't delay them any longer.

Senchi: Why, I smelled something all right. What are they? Your acolytes? Wait a minute. They're in mourning. Is someone dead? [*To Edufa*] None of your own, I hope.

Edufa: No.

Chorus: This was an old sorrow, friend.

Senchi: Ah! I understand. One of those 'condolence' rites. Why do you people prolong your sorrows so? [*To Chorus*] Though, I must observe, you have a funny way of going about it, drinking and sniggering. [*Very playfully*] Come on, give me those confounded sticks. I'll show you what they are good for. [*He snatches the clappers from the Chorus, and a mock chase follows during which he tries to smack them. He flings the clappers in a heap below the steps near the kitchen*] Now, embrace me, and be done with sorrow.

Chorus: [*Delighted*] Oh! Oh! We were on our way.

Senchi: To me.

[*Seguwa entering, sees the romping, and her single exclamation is both disapproving and full of anxiety. Senchi turn to her*]

What's the matter with the mother pussy cat? Come over lady and join the fun.

Edufa:	[*Sensitive to Seguwa's disapproval*] Let the women go now, Senchi.
Senchi:	Why? That's no way to treat me.
Seguwa:	[*Ominously*] Edufa.
Edufa:	They can come back some other time.
Senchi:	Tonight? All of them?
Seguwa:	Edufa.
Edufa:	Let them go now. Tonight? Very well, tonight.
Chorus three:	[*Eagerly*] To eat?
Seguwa:	Edufa.
Edufa:	Yes. Why not?
Senchi:	You mean that?
Edufa:	A bit of a party, since my wife recovers…and …
Senchi:	Oh, how thoughtless of me. Has Ampoma been ill? And I haven't asked of her … though I've brought her a song. It's all your fault for distracting me. Sorry.
Edufa:	… and you too have come, my friend, and brought us luck, it seems to me that we are permitted to celebrate my good fortune…
Chorus One:	Expect us.
Chorus Two:	We will be glad to help you celebrate.
Edufa:	[*To Chorus*] … and to you also I owe my gratitude…
Chorus:	Expect us.
	[*They leave cheerfully through the gate*]
Senchi:	Wonderful.

[*He joins Edufa in the court*]

Edufa:	[*With a great sigh*] Oh, Senchi! This has been quite a day.
Senchi:	[*Suddenly serious*] Tired? Between you and me, my friend, I'm downright weary in my b-o-n-e-s myself. I've become quite a wanderer, you know, tramping out my life. It isn't as if I didn't know what I'm looking for. I do. But oh, the bother and the dither. And the

	pushing and the jostling. Brother, if you meet one kind, loving person in this world who will permit a fellow to succeed at something good and clean, introduce me; for I would wish to be his devotedly and positively forever. Amen, But of that, more later. I'm worn out with travel. Lead me to a bed in a quiet corner, for some sweet, friendly, uncompleted sleep.
Edufa:	Won't you eat?
Senchi:	No food. Only peace, for a while.
Edufa:	As you wish. [*To Seguwa*] Take my friend to the guest rooms overlooking the river. It's quiet there. We'll talk when you awake. No luggage?
Senchi:	[*Showing his battered leather case*] This is all I care about.
Edufa:	[*To Seguwa*] See that he has all the needs. And after, arrange a meal for tonight. Spare nothing. [*He hurries into his rooms*]
Seguwa:	[*Grimly*] This way.

[*She strides ahead to the steps leading into the guest rooms*]

Senchi:	[*Catching up with her*] For the sake of a man's nerves, can't you smile? I can't stand gloom.
Seguwa:	You should have your fun another day.
Senchi:	What particular brand of fun is this you're recommending?
Seguwa:	The party tonight.
Senchi:	That? Don't call that a party, woman. Call it something like Senchi's Temporary Plan for the Prevention of Senchi from Thinking Too Hard. You don't grudge me a small relief like that, surely.

[*Seguwa wipes away a tear*]

35

Come on. Now what have I said? Are you one of those women who enjoy crying? I'll make a bargain with you, then. Allow me to have my rest. When I awake, I promise to make you cry to your heart's content — by singing, merely. I make songs, you know. [*Patting his leather case*] Songs for everything: songs for goodness, songs for badness, for strength, for weakness; for dimples, and wrinkles; — and, for making you cry. But I'll tell you a secret. I never make songs about ugliness because I simply think it should not exist.

Seguwa: [*Exasperated*] this way, please.

[*She leads Senchi up the steps*]
[*Abena enters from the kitchen with a smart tray on which it a hot dish of soup. She is on her way to Edufa's rooms, looking decidedly happy*]

Abena: [*Stopping halfway up the steps, proudly smelling the soup*] She will like it. I used only aromatic peppers — the yellow— and the mint smells good.
[*Edufa comes out*] Dear brother.
[*She raises the tray for him to smell the soup*]

Edufa: [*Smelling*] Lovely. Little one, are you well? We haven't talked much of late.

Abena: I'm glad she's better.

Edufa: Oh…yes. You did your work well, it seems.

Abena: My work?

Edufa: [*Quickly changing the subject*] How is your young man? [*He takes the tray*]

Abena: [*Shyly*] I will see him today.

Edufa: Good. You haven't had much of a chance lately, have you?

Abena: No… er … Can't I take the soup in to her? I've had such thoughts. I miss her. We were so happy before all

this began; stringing beads and looking through her clothes. She's going to let me wear her long golden chain of miniature barrels at my wedding — right down to my feet.

Edufa: Let's get her up strong, then. You can see her tonight. We have guests.

Abena: [*Appreciatingly*] yes. I've heard him singing.

Edufa: It's very good to have him here.

Abena: He sings well.

Edufa: Some women from town are coming to eat with us tonight.

Abena: [*With childlike joy*] People here again. Laughter again.

Edufa: [*Smiling, but compelling her down the steps*]
Sister. Come. [*Intimately*] Did you mind staying up at nights? Was it very hard?

Abena: [*Unburdening*] Not...too...hard. I didn't mind it inside the house, though it got so ghostly quiet at times, I almost saw my lonely thoughts talking shape before my eyes...becoming form in the empty air. And then, collecting the stream water... that ... that in the night, and the forest such a crowd of unfamiliar presences.

Edufa: Hush! It's over. All over. Thank you. Go out now. Enjoy yourself. Can you give us a nice meal tonight?

Abena: Delighted.

[*As she goes through the kitchen door, Sam enters through the gate, running, dodging, like one pursued. He carries a bird cage and a small tin box*]

Sam: [*To an imaginary crowd towards the gate*]
Thank you. Thank you. [*Gloatingly*] They didn't get me. [*Speaking to no one in particular*] an idiot's life isn't so bad. There are always people to stop children throwing stones at us. They only do that for idiots, I find. [*To the cage*] Let us tell my master that.

[*Paying tender attention to what is inside the cage, he walks up a step, crosses to left, and puts the cage and the box down*]

Seguwa: [*Entering from the kitchen*] you're back.
Sam: Are you pleased to see me? [*Lifting up the cage*] Look, he is my bird.
Seguwa: [*Horrified*] don't bring it near me. It's an owl.
Sam: [*Blithely*] Of course. An owl is a bird.
Seguwa: What's it doing here?
Sam: It came with me. It was an owl before, but now it's with me, it's no longer itself. It's the owl of an idiot. What we get, we possess. I caught it in a tree.
Seguwa: Take it outside. [*Sam sulks, turning his back on her*] Did everything go well? Did you find the place? Did you see the man? [*Sam moving his bird cage outside, merely nods his affirmatives*] And what's the news? [*Sams back stiffens stubbornly*] It's no good, he won't talk to me. I'll let your master know you're back.

[*She goes into Edufa's rooms, while Sam pays fussy attention to his owl. She returns with Edufa who is in a state of high expectancy*]

            There he is … back.
Edufa: [*Coaxingly*] Sam, are you back?
Seguwa: I don't know what he's doing with that thing. Let him take it away.
Edufa: What is it, Sam?
Seguwa: An owl.
Edufa: [*Terrified*] Take it out. [*Sam sulks*] We would do well not to disturb him before we've heard what he has to say. He can get very stubborn. [*Sweetly*] Sam, come here. [*Sam doesn't budge*] You may keep your bird. [*Sam turns to him grinning broadly*]

Sam: [*Pointing to the owl*] M owl and I had a nice thought for you on the way. When you are born again, master, why don't you come back as an idiot? There are always people to stop children throwing stones at us. They only do that for idiots, I find.

Edufa: [*Smiling in spite of himself*] All right. Now tell me quickly what I want to know. [*Anxiously*] did you find the place?

Sam: It's an awful place. What do you send me to places like that for? Not the village itself. That is beautiful, floating in blue air on the mountain top, with a climb-way in the mountain's belly going zig-zag-zig, like a game.

[*He thoroughly enjoys his description*]

Seguwa: [*Impatiently*] He's so tiresome with his rambling

Edufa: [*Trying to be patient*] Good, you found the village. And the man?

Sam: He is a nice man, tall as a god. And he fed me well. You don't give me chicken to eat, but he did. [*Thinks a bit*] What does such a nice man live in an awful house like that for? That's the awful part.

Edufa: [*very anxiously*] Never mind. What did he say?

Sam: Ah! [*Secretively*] Let me fetch my box of goods.

[*He fetches the tin box and sets it down before Edufa*]

First, three pebbles from the river. [*He takes out these pebbles*]
Catch them. [*He throws them one by one to Edufa*]
One, Two, Three.

[*Edufa catches them all*]

Good! They didn't fall.

Edufa: [*Intensely*] I understand that. We mustn't let Ampoma fall to the ground.

Sam: [*Taking out a ball of red stuff*] With this, make the sign of the sun on your doorstep where you spirit walks in and out with you. Come, I know you are not much of an artist. I'll do it for you the way the man showed me.

              [*He walks importantly to the step leading to Edufa's rooms, and as he draws a raying sun boldly on the riser or the first step*]

              Rays! Everywhere … you … turn.

Seguwa: [*With awe*] Ampoma talks so much of the sun.

Edufa: Yearningly.

Sam: [*Returning to the box*] And then came the part I didn't understand.

Edufa: [*Hoarsely*] Yes… quickly, where is it?

Sam: Here it is in this bag.
              [*He produces an old leather pouch which is spectacularly designed and hung with small talismans*]

Edufa: [*Trembling*] give it to me.

Sam: Now listen. He says burn it.
              [*Edufa snatches the pouch from him*]

Edufa: [*To Seguwa*] Get fire — in the back courtyard. Quickly. [*Seguwa leaves in haste*]

Sam: [*With emphasis*] The man says, burn it with your own hands, before you bathe in the herbs for the last time.

Edufa: [*Eyes shut*] We're saved. [*When he becomes aware again of the waiting Sam*] Well done, Sam. You may go.

Sam: I won't go to that awful house again.

Edufa: No. Get something to eat. And rest. You are tired.
              [*Sam picks up the box and walks eagerly to the bird's cage*]

	But… Sam. You must let that bird go.
Sam:	[*Aggrieved*] My owl? Oh, master, he is my friend. He's the bird of an idiot. He likes us. He and I had a nice thought for you on our way…
Edufa:	[*Threateningly*] Take it out of here! Out.
Sam:	Oh… [*He picks up the bird cage and goes out of the gate muttering sulkily*] We'll stay outside… If they won't have us in, we won't eat… We will starve ourselves… we…
Edufa:	[*Gripping the pouch in his fists with violence*] This is the final act. I will turn chance to certainly. I will burn this horror charm, and bury its ashes in the ground; the one act that was still hazard if left undone.

Scene One

[*A trestle table covered with a fresh white cloth is moved into the court, close to the central seat. So is a loaded drinks trolley. The seats left, and right, are shifted in. Wicker garden chairs provide additional seating. Abena and Seguwa are preparing for the party, obviously enjoying doing it with some taste. They move in plates, cutlery, serviettes, wine glasses, etc: pursuing their work without paying more than momentary attention to any distractions*].

[*Senchi and Edufa appear from the guest rooms. Edufa is in evening dress, but has yet to put on his jacket. Senchi looks noticeably absurd in a suit that is not his size. He brings his leather case which he soon places carefully against the trestle table*]

Senchi: I'm grateful to you for listening to all my talk.

Edufa: If it helps, I'm happy to listen. What can I do more?

Senchi: Every now and then I feel this urge to talk to somebody. It helps me to dispose of the dust of my experience. And that's when I come here. There are not many people with enough concern to care about what accumulate inside a man. [*He indicates his heart*] You and Ampoma both listen well, though I must say that you being so solid and so unemotional, lack the rain of her sympathy.

Edufa: That's your secret, then. I've never told you I admire you although you can't show a balance in the bank, have I?

Senchi: No.

Edufa: I do. You're so relaxed, and normally so convincing with your laughter. Yet, you do puzzle me somewhat. Don't you think it is important to have solidity? Be something? Somebody is being merely alive not senseless?

Senchi: What is this something, this somebody that you are? Give it name and value. I'm not being disparaging; I'm seeking.

Edufa: I don't know. I thought I did until it got so confusing, I… Ask the town. They know who Edufa is and what he's worth. They can count you out my value in the homes that eat because I live. Yes, my enterprises feed them. They rise in deference, from their chairs when they say my name. if that isn't something, what is? And can a man allow himself to lose grip on that? Let it go? A position like that? You want to maintain it with substance, protect it from ever present envy with vigilance. And there's the strain that rips you apart! The pain of holding on to what you have. It gives birth to fears which pinch at the heart and dement the mind, until you needs must clutch at some other faith… Oh, it has driven me close to horror… and I tell you, I don't know what to think now.

Senchi: [*Who has been listening with concern*]
We make an odd pair of friends, to be sure. You, with your machines growling at granite in your quarries to crumble and deliver to you their wealth; and I, trying to pay my way in the currency of my songs. But perhaps, that, like many statements we are capable of expressing, is merely grasping at extremes of light and dark, and missing the subtle tones for which we haven't yet found words.

Edufa: Yes, I do have my moments when I'm not quite as solid as you think; when solidity becomes illusory.

Senchi: But you do give an impression of being settled and satisfied, which is what I'm not.

Edufa: I wish I could, like you, dare to bare myself for scrutiny. [*Pause*] I'm being compelled to learn however, and the day will come, I suppose.

Senchi: Ah, yes. We commit these thoughts to the wind and leave it to time to sift them. [*Snapping out of his serious mood*] I'm ready for immediacy, which is this evening's light relief. Where are the ladies?

Edufa: Don't worry; they will not miss this chance to dine at Edufa's house.

Senchi: [*Preening*] Do I look noticeable? [*Making much of his ill-fitting suit*] I've never gone hunting in fancy dress before.

Edufa: [*Really laughing*] Oh, Senchi, you're so refreshing, you ass.

Senchi: Yes, call me ass. Always, it's "You're an ass!" Seldom does a man say, "I am an ass." That takes courage. But you're right. I am an ass, or I would be wearing my own suit.

Edufa: Come on. You don't mind wearing my suit?

Senchi: I do. It's the same as a borrowed song, to me. Singing other people's songs, or wearing other people's suits, neither suits me.

Edufa: [*Teasing*] well, you're in it now.

Senchi: Being an ass, I am. However, it will serve for an evening of foolery. [*A flash of seriousness again*] Tell me, do you understand, though?

Edufa: What, Senchi?

Senchi: [*Earnestly*] you see, it's like this. My own suit may be shabby, but its shabbiness is of my making. I understand it. It is a guide to self evaluation. When I stand in it, I know where I stand and why. And that, strangely, means to me dignity and security.

Edufa: There, you're getting very serious. Have a drink.

Senchi: A drink. Ah, yes. [*Stopping short at the trolley*] Oh, no, not before I have greeted Ampoma with breath that I have freshened in my sleep. [*He sits. Edufa serves himself a drink*]

Scene Two

Edufa:	Our guests will soon arrive. Before they do, I have an act of love that I must make tonight.
Senchi:	You surprise me. Can't you wait? You?
Edufa:	It is a gesture of pure pleasure such as my heart has never before requested.
Senchi:	I don't need telling about the pleasure of it. What I'm saying is, Can't you wait? You?
Edufa:	Just now, you judged me unemotional.
Senchi:	Don't worry; after this confessional, I absolve you of the charge.
Edufa:	You see, I've never stinted in giving my wife gifts. Gold she has, and much that money can buy. But tonight, I'm a man lifted up by her love, and I know that nothing less than flowers will do for one such as she is.
Senchi:	Applause. Talk on.
Edufa:	[*To Abena*] Fetch the flowers, sister.

[*She goes into the kitchen*]

Senchi:	[*Watching her go*] You make me feel so unmarried; confusing Senchi's plan for the Ruination of Women. You're driving me to sell my freedom to the next girl that comes too near me.
Edufa:	Don't do that. Learn to love, my friend.

[*Abena returns with a beautiful bouquet of fresh flowers and hands it to Edufa*]

Senchi:	Lovely.
Edufa:	[*To Abena*] Little one, you who are soon to marry, I'm giving you a chance to look at love. Take these flowers in to Ampoma. [*He speaks emotionally into the flowers*] Tell her, that I, her husband, send them;

that it is she who has so matured my love. I would have presented them myself, but I have learned the magic of shyness, and haven't the boldness to look into her eyes yet. [*Abena embraces him happily and takes the flowers from him*]

Senchi: Applause! Standing ovation! This is the first graceful act I've ever seen you do. [*As Abena walks away*] Keep the door open as you go, and let my song keep tune to this moment of nobility. [*He sings*]
Nne
Nne Nne
Nne
Nne Nne
O, Mother
Nne
Nne Nne

[*Abena turning in appreciation of the song, drops the flowers which fall on the step with the sign of the sun on it*]

Abena: Oh! [*She quickly retrieves the flowers*]
Edufa: [*Becoming tense*] For God's sake be careful.
Senchi: [*Continuing after the incident*]
If I find you
Nne
Nne Nne
I'll have to worship you
Nne
Nne Nne
I must adore you
Nne
Nne Nne
O mother
Nne
Nne Nne

[*Edufa, enchanted by the song, attempts to join quietly in the refrain*]

She's wonderful
She's wonderful
O, Mother
She's wonderful
Yes, if I find you
Nne
Nne Nne
I'll have to worship you
Nne
Nne Nne

I must adore you
Nne
Nne Nne
O Mother
Nne
Nne Nne

Edufa: Very good, Senchi.

[*Seguwa is so affected by the song that she is sobbing quietly behind the table*]

Senchi: [*Noticing her*] That is the wettest-eyed woman I've ever seen. [*He goes to her*] Oh, sorry; I promised to make you cry, didn't I? There now, are you happy?
Seguwa: That's a song after my own heart.
Senchi: After mine also.

[*There is a sudden ripple of laughter from Edufa's rooms*]

Edufa: [*Elatedly*] That is her laughter. That is Ampoma. I lover her. [*Abena returns*] Is she happy?

Abena: Radiant. She was standing before the mirror when I entered, looking at her image, her clothes laid out on the bed beside her. Seeing the flowers mirrored there with her, she turned to greet their brightness with her laughter. Then she listened to your song with her eyes shut, and sighed a happy sigh. She listened to your message attentively and said, "Tell my husband that I understand."

Edufa: [*Glowing*] She does. I know. She loves. I know.

Abena: "Tell Senchi", she said, "that all will be left to those who dare to catch in song the comfort of this world."

Senchi: That, I have understood.

Abena: And she will join you later, she says.

Edufa: Yes, she is able to, tonight. Great heartbeat of mine, it is good to be alive. [*Briskly*] Senchi, a drink now?

[*They go to the drinks*]

Abena: Everything is ready to serve, brother. And I am awaited.

Edufa: [*Affectionately*] Go, you have earned your moment.

[*Abena hurries out*]

Senchi: [*Watching her approvingly*] Little sister, buxom sister. I ought to think of marrying that girl.

Edufa: [*Smiling*] Too late. You have lost her to another.

Senchi: Too bad. I'm always ending up blank. But, never mind now. [*Declaiming*] I will make do with ephemerals. Turn up the next page in Senchi's chronicle of uncertainties. [*He gets a drink*]

Scene Three

Senchi:	[*At the trolley, his back on the courtyard*] They are coming.
Edufa:	[*Turning round and seeing nobody*] How do you know?
Senchi:	[*Also turning round*] I'm highly sensitized, that's all. I can feel women twenty miles away minimum range.

[*The Chorus enter through the gate, talking. They are dressed, even overdressed for the evening*]

Chorus One:	That was exciting, dodging those prying eyes in town.
Edufa:	[*To Senchi*] You win. They are here.
Chorus Two:	Won't they be surprised tomorrow when they learn that we too have been invited here.
Chorus Three:	There they are, waiting for us.
Senchi:	[*To Edufa, meaning his suit*] Do I look noticeable?
Edufa:	[*Sharing the fun*] I don't stand a chance beside you.
Chorus One:	How do I look?
Chorus Four:	Fine. [*With relish*] Look at that table. It is good simply to see.
Chorus Two:	[*Also impressed*] Ei!
Senchi:	Is there a roadblock there? Come on, I never allow women to keep me waiting.
Chorus:	[*In fun below the courtyard steps*] Is there anybody in this beautiful house?
Senchi:	[*Pleased*] A lively flock, eh? They have a sense of humour. That's a good beginning.
Edufa:	[*Coming forward*] Good evening.
Chorus:	We answer you.
Senchi:	[*Meeting them*] Embrace me.
Chorus One:	[*Flirtatiously*] Do you always do things in such a hurry?

Senchi: That's a good one. That is a rollicking good one. Lady, for that much perkiness, I'm yours… momentarily.

Edufa: [*Enjoying it*] Senchi. Ladies, it's very good of you to come and thank you for this morning's kindness.

Chorus One: We trust your wife keeps well. Shall we be seeing her this evening?

Edufa: Certainly. She will join you presently.

Chorus One: Accept this little gift for her from all of us here. [*She hands the gift to him*]

Chorus Two: We were making so much noise here this morning; we hope we didn't disturb her in any serious way.

Edufa: Oh, no. On her behalf, I thank you. Sit wherever you like.

[*The Chorus choose seats. Chorus Four sits close to the set table, eyeing everything*]

This is indeed most pleasant. I'll get you drinks.
[*He places the gift on the table and gets busy with drinks*]

Senchi: [*Startling Chorus Four at the table*] We are not quite eating yet, you know.

Chorus Four: [*Naively*] It looks so pretty.

Senchi: You look prettier than forks and knives and stiff backed serviettes; that is sure.

Chorus Four: [*Uncomprehending*] Serviettes?

Senchi: Yes, these things. [*Taking her by the hand to the seat near the kitchen*] Sit over here with me. I have other things I rather think it will be interesting to try to negotiate with you. May I hold your hand? Or is that considered adultery in these parts? [*They sit*] I always try to get the local customs straight before I begin negotiations.

Edufa: [*Handling our drinks*] Senchi, give the lady a drink at least.

[*Senchi assists him*]

Chorus Four: Lady! Ei, that's nice.
Senchi: [*Pleased with her*] She is positively c-u-t-e.
Chorus Two: [*Confidentially to Chorus Three*] This is all as we
               imagined it. Better even.
Chorus Three: [*Full of curiosity*] Who is his friend?
Senchi: [*At the trolley*] Aha! I have ears like a hare, you
               know. Before a woman can say 'Sench', I come to the
               summons of her thought. I'm acutely sensitive. Edufa,
               she wants to know who I am. Tell her I'm a neo-
               millionaire in search of underdeveloped territories.
               [*The Chorus responds with laughter*]
               They applaud. They do have a sense of humour. Fine.
               [*Fussily*] Drinks all round, and who cares which is
               what. [*He hands a drink to Chorus Four*]

Edufa: I do. Everyone gets exactly what she wants.

               [*The drinks are settled. Senchi sits in a central position*]

Senchi: [*Raising his glass ceremoniously*] Wc have it in hand
               [*A moment of awkward silence, as people drink*]
               Now, what's the silence for? This is a party. Shall we
               play games?
Chorus One: What games?
Senchi: Party games.
Edufa: Excuse me. I'll see if Ampoma is ready. [*He goes to his
               rooms*]
Senchi: [*Rising promptly*] That's kind of you, Edufa. [*To
               Chorus*] He is a most consideration, kind-hearted
               man when I'm around.
               Let's make the best of our opportunities. Now,
               let me see. We will not play Musical Chairs; that
               being a little colonial is somewhat inappropriate

	here… But, I'm open to suggestion… and … if you like, inspection too. [*Chorus laugh heartily as he strikes poses*] They merely laugh — which is no way to encourage me. Hm…[*He plays at thinking seriously*] Do you like songs?
Chorus:	[*Enthusiastically*] Yes.
Senchi:	[*Liking this*] That means I can entertain you in songs, eh?
Chorus:	Yes.
Senchi:	Do you like stories?
Chorus:	Yes.
Senchi:	That means I must tell them, eh?
Chorus:	Yes.
Senchi:	What do I get for all of this, from you?
Chorus One:	We laugh for you.
Senchi:	And with me?
Chorus:	Oh, yes.
Senchi:	Yes, Yes. Do you never say no?
Chorus:	No
Senchi:	Brilliant conversation. Senchi, you must make better headway. [*Pauses reflectively*] Oh, yes you are. They say they don't ever say no.
Chorus One:	Isn't he funny!

[*She and the others have been enjoying a private joke centred on Senchi's ill-fitting suit*]

Senchi:	Oh, madam, that's unkind.
Chorus One:	It's your suit…pardon me… but your suit…
Senchi:	That kind of joke should thoroughly frustrate a man. But I must admit it is most intelligent of you. I don't know whether you realize how positively brilliant your observation is. Well now, what next? I have an idea. I sing a bit, you know.
Chorus:	[*Eagerly*] Ah!

Senchi: Does that mean, 'Sing'?
Chorus: Yes.
Senchi: Yes! We will all sing my song. Listen, it's easy. [*He sings snatches of the song for Ampoma, encouraging the Chorus to participate. They try*]
Chorus One: It's sad.
Senchi: So it is. But quickly before you start crying all over me, here is a rumpus song all right. We will have the foolery for which I'm fitly suited tonight. Here is the story of it. A traveller's tale. I'm a bit of a traveller, you know. [*He poses for effect*]

And I came to this city called Bam, and there was this man; whether he is mad or simply stark raving poor, I couldn't ascertain. But he impressed me, I can tell you that. Wait a minute, I've written his story down. [He takes some sheets of paper out of his leather bag] I'm a bit of a writer, you know. [*The Chorus nudge each other*]

A man claimed insane walks through the city streets. No prophet nor priest costumed in fancy gown is he; but he too, a fire with zeal, feels that men must heed his creed; or at the least applaud the wit with which he calls them sons of a bitch.

[*He looks round for approval. The faces round him are getting blank with incomprehension. He becomes more declamatory*]

He raves through the city streets at sane passer-by. And what does he say? He feels that heed ought to be given to his preaching, or at the least, applause must greet his singular screeching:

'Gentlemen', show me a thought you've thought through, and I'll bow to you right low and grant you a master's due.

'Feather-fine ladies' with hips that rhyme, who the blazes minds your children's manners at this time?

'Left, right, left, does not feed a nation. I'd rather have you roaring drunk at a harvest celebration'.

Oh, he is a character, an absolute word — exhibitor. But, ladies, where is your laughter? Aren't you amused?

Chorus: [*Quite blank*] We are listening.

Senchi: Good. I thought myself that his words should sound good on a trumpet. [*He takes a small trumpet out of his leather case*]
Come on, procession!

[*He begins to blow a tune to the words in quotation above. The Chorus are swept into the fun. They are dancing round after him, procession style, when Edufa enters, now in his jacket*]

Join up Edufa. Procession.

[*Edufa complete. Senchi alternates between the trumpet and singing the words. Presently, the whole group is singing to his accompaniment. Ampoma appears unnoticed at the top of the steps. She is tastefully dressed in a delicate colour, looking very much like a bride. She watches the romping scene briefly with a mixture of sadness and amusement, before she descends at a point when the group is taking a turn in the courtyard*]

Edufa: [*Seeing her*] Ah, friends, my wife!

[*The singing and dancing comes to an abrupt halt*]

Senchi: [*With profound admiration*] Ampoma. Mother.

Chorus:	Beautiful.
Ampoma:	[*Graciously*] I'm sorry I was not up to welcome you, Senchi.
Senchi:	You are here now, Ampoma, and well. I couldn't wish for more.
Ampoma:	That was your singing. It is a lovely song.
Senchi:	Yes, for such as you a man must sing. The song is yours, made in the strain of your name; my gift to you. [*He takes a sheet of music out of his pocket*] Take it. [*She does*] And accept me as yours, devotedly and positively forever... Amen!

[*The Chorus practically applauds*]

Chorus One:	Isn't he a character!
Ampoma:	[*To the chorus*] I didn't know about the women being here. Thank you for your company. I hope my husband is honouring your presence here.
Chorus:	We are most happy to be here.
Edufa:	There, is a gift they brought for you.
Ampoma:	How kind. [*Pensively*] So many rays of kindness falling on me, each with its own intensity... [*Brightening*] I respond with warm heart... and hand. [*She shakes hands hurriedly and nervously with the Chorus*]
Edufa:	[*Whispering to her*] your hand is trembling. You're sure you're not cold? I'll fetch you a wrap.
Ampoma:	[*With cheerfulness*] No, I'm well wrapped in your affection, and that is warm enough. My friends, you see I have a most affectionate husband.
Senchi:	We will have to name this the night of fond declarations.
Edufa:	[*A little nervously*] had we better eat now?
Ampoma:	Yes, our friends must be hungry... and it is getting late.
Senchi:	Escort her to her chair there.

[*He starts the Chorus singing again and moving in mock procession into the court. Ampoma joins in the game. Suddenly, she loses her balance and barely avoids a fall. Only her hand touches the ground as she steadies herself*]

Senchi: [*Springing to her support*] Oh, sorry.

Edufa: [*Worried*] Be careful with her. [*He escorts her to a chair by the pillar*] Sit down, Ampoma, please. [*Seguwa who sees the fall as she is bringing in a dish of food is frozen is her track. This so unnerves Edufa, that he speaks harshly to her*] Where's the food? Why are you standing there? Bring it. [*He gives attention to Ampoma*]

Ampoma: I'm all right. Please don't shout at her. She has nursed me well.

Senchi: No, Edufa, don't. That woman's tears are too ready to fall.

[*From this stage, a strange mood develops in Ampoma. She frequently talks like one whose mind is straying*]

Ampoma: [*Fast*] Friends, eat. My husband provides well. I hope you're happy here. Why am I sitting down? [*She rises*] I must feed you. [*As she quickly passes plates of food served by Seguwa*] Eat. We must eat to keep the body solidly on its feet. I wasn't able to cook for you myself. [*Pause*] That's sad. A woman must serve her husband well. But I'm sure the food is good. We never serve anything but the best to our friends. Eat. You don't know how good it was to hear you fill this house with merriment. Eat.

[*Everyone is served. She sits down, and receives a plate from Edufa who has been watching her anxiously*]

Senchi: [*To Chorus Four*] You may eat now.

[*Edufa sits down beside Ampoma but his mind is not on his food*]

Ampoma, I need your rare counsel. Which of these five women shall I take to wife, lawfully?

Ampoma: [*Laughing gaily*] Oh, Senchi, bless you. Which one catches your eye everywhere you turn, like I catch Edufa's eye? That's the one you should have.

[*The women avert their eyes, eating busily*]

Senchi: [*Looking round*] No hope.
Edufa: [*At the table*] Here is wine. [*Like one about to propose a toast*] This evening is a celebration unpremeditated.
Senchi: [*Sitting up*] Speak, husband, speak.
Edufa: There is nowhere I would rather be, nothing more than this I would rather be doing. Join with me in drinking to the health of my lovely wife, whom I publicly proclaim a woman among women, and friend among friends.
Senchi: Applause. Vote of thanks!
Edufa: Drink. To her health.
Chorus and Senchi: [*Rising glass in hand*] To your health, Ampoma.
Chorus One: [*Instinctively formal*] In all directions we let our libation pour. Your husband is true and rare. Live together blessedly to the end of your days. Health to you.
Chorus: Health to your children. Health to your house.
Ampoma: [*Deeply shaken*] I will have some wine now. Thank you, my friends.

Edufa: [*Serving her*] Here.
Senchi: And enough of solemnity. You're making her pensive.

[*They all sit*]

Edufa: [*With unconcealed concern*] Ampoma.
Ampoma: I'm all right. [*She rises. She is not all right*]
                It is a moving thing to feel a prayer poured into your
                soul. But now it's over. [*Pause*] Give me some wine
                [*Now straining for a diversion, she moves forward
                to gaze into the sky above the courtyard*] The night
                is usually full of stars. Where are they all tonight?
                Senchi, can't you sing them out in a riot?
Senchi: [*Beside her, parodying*] Little stars; little, colossal, little
                stars. How I wonder where you are. How I wonder
                why you are. How I wonder which one of you is my
                star; and why you fizzle.
Ampoma: [*Very pleased*] That's good. Oh, Senchi.
Chorus One: He is never at a loss for things to say.
Chorus Two: It's extraordinary.
Edufa: If he could settle down he could become a poet.
Ampowa: [*Seriously*] He is one already, no matter how he roams.
Senchi: [*Touched*] Thank you, Ampoma.
Ampoma: [*Returning to her chair*] Eat, friends, it's late.
Chorus Two: But you are not eating.
Ampoma: I have fed all I need. And there is no time.
                Very soon, I must embrace my husband before you
                all, answering the affection into which he draws me.
                [*She rises hastily and loses her balance again, just
                avoiding a fall, steadying herself with her hand*]
Edufa: [*Supporting her, and very disturbed*] Don't trouble, I
                implore you.
Senchi: [*To Ampoma*] Sorry. [*Trying to relax the tensing
                atmosphere*] But, come on Edufa. Let her embrace
                you. I haven't ever seen Ampoma breaking through

	her shyness. Besides, if she embraces you, then I can embrace all the others; and so the night makes progress swingingly.
Ampoma:	[*Embracing Edufa*] Women, I hope you don't think me without modesty. [*Taking up a position*] We spend most of our days preventing the heart from beating out its greatness. The things we would rather encourage lie choking among the weeds of our restrictions. And before we know it, time has eluded us. There is not much time allotted us, and half of that we sleep. While we are awake we should allow our hearts to beat without shame of being seen living. [*She looks magnificent and quite aloof. Then more quietly*]

My husband, you have honoured me by your words and by your precious gift of flowers. I wish to honour you in return, in language equally unashamed. [*She beckons to Seguwa who since her near fall, has been expressing her alarm in the background*]

Go to my room. On my bed there is a casket. Bring it to me. [*Seguwa complies*] |
| Chorus Two: | Many women would like to be in a position to say what you have said here, Ampoma. |
| Senchi: | Therefore, I should not neglect to pay attention to my preliminary surveys which will prepare the way for such contracts to be signed. [*He eyes the Chorus playfully*] shall we change seats? [*As he changes seats to sit by another woman*] I have been camping too long in one place and getting nowhere. |

[*Seguwa returns with the casket*]

Edufa:	[*Confused and uncomfortable*] what's this?
Ampoma:	[*Opening the casket and taking out some smart waist beads*] Waist beads, bearing the breath of my tenderness.

Chorus:	[*Non-plussed, eyes popping, but laughing*] Oh!Oh!
Edufa:	[*Astounded, embarrassed, but not displeased*] Ampoma!
Senchi:	[*Beside himself*] Great! Whew!
Ampoma:	[*Inscrutable*] Women, you understand, don't you, that with this, I mean to claim him mine. And you are witnesses. My husband, wear this with honour. [*She surprises Edufa by slipping the beads round his neck. His first reaction is of shock*] With it, I declare to earth and sky and water, and all things with which we shall soon be one, that I am slave to your flesh and happy so to be. Wear it proudly, this symbol of the union of our flesh. [*The Chorus and Senchi are making the best of a most astonishing situation, by laughing at Edufa's discomfiture*]
Edufa:	[*Attempting to hide his embarrassment behind a smile*] Why Ampoma… well… what can I say… [*He removes the beads as soon as she lets go*]
Senchi:	That's rich. Oh, Ampoma, you are the most terrific woman I have ever seen. Don't stand there so foolishly, Edufa. Do something. Say something. I would sweep her up in my arms, take wings and be gone.
Ampoma:	[*Very abruptly*] Excuse me, friends, I must leave you. I hope you will tell the town what I have done without considering it gossip. If I had wished it not to be known, I would not have done it here before you. Take my hand in yours, quickly. [*She shakes hands with the women in great haste*] I am happy that you came… I do not know you well, but you are women and you give me boldness to commit my deepest feelings to your understanding. [*She is hurrying away*] Sleep well when you return to your own homes.

Chorus:	[*Chilled*] Goodnight, Ampoma. Goodnight
Edufa:	[*Miserably*] I must see her in. [*He catches up with her before she reaches the steps*] Are you all right?
Ampoma:	[*Brightly*] Oh, yes. It's such a relief to feel so well at last. [*She takes his hand, looks round, and seems to be wanting to linger. Edufa attempts to lead her away*]
Senchi:	[*To Chorus*] You have seen truth.
Chorus One:	I couldn't have believed it if my own eyes hadn't witnessed it. Ampoma?
Senchi:	Just do what she recommends, that's all.

[*Edufa and Ampoma are going up the steps*]

Ampoma:	Thank you, but don't leave our friends. I want to go in alone.
Edufa:	As you wish, my dear, but…
Ampoma:	I want to; please don't leave them now.
Edufa:	[*Reluctantly*] I'll make it very brief and join you presently. [*He comes down*] Ah, Senchi, she's all but taken my breath away.

[*Ampoma falls on the step with the sign of the sun on it, causing Seguwa to scream. Edufa runs to her, yelling with horror*]

	No! Ampoma! No!
Senchi:	[*Helping to lift up Ampoma*] Why didn't you take her up the steps?
Chorus Two:	She's been unsteady all the time. She's not recovered yet, is she?
Edufa:	[*Unaware of anyone else's presence*] There, Ampoma, there. You didn't fall all the way to the ground. I will not let you fall. No! No! No! Not to the ground. To the ground? No! Lean on me. You

shouldn't have come out. I shouldn't have permitted it. Oh! No!

[*He is taking her up*]

Senchi: [*With great concern*] Take her in. It wasn't a big fall, fortunately. [*Helplessly*] sleep well, Ampoma. [*Ampoma turns to look at him with a wistful smile. He is left standing alone on the steps, deeply puzzled*]
That's strange… [*He comes down*] Well, sit down ladies. [*Obviously trying to pretend the atmosphere of panic doesn't exist*] I don't blame Edufa for overdoing his concern. He's a man caught in the spell of high romance. Why, if I were in his shoes I would be even more wildly solicitous. [*He thinks this over, forgetting the presence of the Chorus meanwhile*] In his shoes? No, not that. I'm wearing his suit, I openly confess, but his shoes I wouldn't wear. I Senchi, must at all times maintain a genuine contact with the basic earth in my own shoes. [*Shaking himself out of his reflections*] Have a drink. [*But he cannot move*] She didn't fall too badly, did she? Perhaps she shouldn't be up yet.

Chorus One: I'm thinking the same, remembering her action here.

Chorus Two: You saw it? The tension beneath the smile?

Chorus Three: She was unhappy.

Chorus One: But she was happy also, strangely.

[*It is now that Seguwa is noticed wandering in the courtyard with gestures of desperation*]

Senchi: [*Unnerved*] Woman, you are too excitable. What are you fussing around like a hen wanting somewhere to lay on egg for?

[*Seguwa looks at him as if she's afraid he'll hit her*]

	Control yourself.
Seguwa:	I cannot anymore. She fell. Did you count? Oh! The thought! She fell three times, and each time she touched the ground, Oh! Oh!

[*The Chorus converges on her*]

Chorus One:	What do you mean?
Senchi:	Oh, come off it. My goodness, she didn't break any bones. Ampoma wouldn't forgive you for making her seem so fragile.
Seguwa:	She fell off the sign of the sun; and the sun itself is blanked and it is dark.
Chorus:	[*With urgency*] What sign?
Seguwa:	[*Out of control*] Bad signs. They would pose no menace if no oath had been sworn, and we were free to read in her present condition, normal disabilities for which remedy is possible. As it is, the reality of that oath makes Edufa for all time guilty, no matter how or when she meets her end.
Senchi:	Don't talk to us in fragments, woman.
Seguwa:	I thought we could cancel out the memory. [*Rushing towards the steps*] But, I see the sign of the three pebbles, and on the third fall she fell on the sign of the sun to the ground. [*She points out the sign of the sun*]
Chorus:	[*Crowding round*] What is it?
Senchi:	What is this, woman?
Seguwa:	[*Hiding her face in her hands and turning away*] It shouldn't be there to plague our memory, deluding us from the path of reason.
Senchi:	This woman is unstable. I wouldn't have her running about my house if I had one. But… what is this sign?
Seguwa:	[*Terrified*] I don't know. I have told you nothing. Get out. I know nothing about it. Why did you come

feasting here tonight? Get out! Get out all of you. [*She rears up against the wall, pointing at the Chorus*] Or, are you eager to take Ampoma's place? Can you pay the price of sharing Edufa's bed? Nothing less than your lives? Oh, he is most dangerous.

[*She dashes off into Edufa's room. The Chorus and Senchi hover round the steps, staring at the sign of the sun*]

Chorus: [*Several voices*] she's terrified.
Senchi: So is Edufa. Does a fall call for these flights of terror? Such hysteria? [*He scrutinizes the sign, and his distress increases*] I should break in there and demand explanation.
Chorus One: Do you remember this morning at our ceremony, that woman's haunted look; her strangeness?
Chorus Two: Her fighting to say whether Edufa was in or out?
Chorus One: And Edufa himself. If there wasn't something terribly wrong, would he have been so conspicuously relieved when Ampoma asked for food?
Senchi: Do you mean that all this happened here?
Chorus Three: Yes, this morning, in our presence.
Senchi: [*Grimly to himself*] To me also, he has shown some strange disturbances of spirit this day… And then, Ampoma's wandering mind tonight, her… But let's not run on so. We know nothing until I go in there.

[*He is about to force his way into Edufa's rooms when Seguwa rushes out. She cringes when she sees him, and flees into the courtyard, her fist in her mouth as if to stifle an outcry*]

Where's Edufa? Woman, speak. What's happening here?

Chorus: Talk to us. Tell us.

                     [*They and Senchi press on Seguwa as she roams with her
                     hand pressed against her mouth. She suddenly notices
                     the clappers the Chorus used in the mourning seizes
                     them, and thrusts them impulsively at the chorus*]

Seguwa: [*Bursting out*] Don't ask me to talk. Help me. You
                     have come to do the rite, have you not? Do it quickly,
                     I implore you.
Senchi: [*At the top of the steps*] Edufa!
Seguwa: What is there left of sacredness?
Chorus: By the souls of our fathers, speak.
Seguwa: It is that evil charm on which the oath was sworn.
                     We cannot ever forget it. We cannot reason without it
                     now.
Senchi: What? Charms in Edufa's house?
Chorus: What charm?
Senchi: Edufa! It's Senchi.
Seguwa: And yet he burned it. But the deed was done. He
                     buried it, but it was her he buried.
Chorus: Buried?
Seguwa: Oh, speak, tongue! Women, you did your ceremony
                     here, but you left the evil one himself behind you.
                     Edufa. He is in there with his victim. This is the day
                     when Edufa should have died. Another has died for
                     him. His wife, Ampoma. She loved him and she has
                     died to spare his life.
Chorus One: Died? For him? People don't die that kind of the
                     death.
Chorus: Died? No. We have eaten here with her, laughed with
                     her.
Senchi: [*Helplessly*] Groans in there…like one who stifles
                     agony lest he sheds unmanly tears. I fear it is the
                     worst, my friends.

Seguwa: Coward! Coward! Coward! He is a cursed man. Go. Tell the town about the man who let his wife die for him. [*She breaks down*] Then go, and tell her mother. Oh, mother! Will someone go and tell her mother, for I cannot look her in the face. I cannot look those motherless children in the face.

Chorus: You lie. We will not believe you.

Seguwa: Come, I'll show you where he buried it.

[*She strides ahead to take them to the back courtyard. Just at this point Edufa comes out, a man clearly going out of his mind. The Chorus runs up to crowd below the steps*]

Chorus One: Oh, Edufa. Has this woman fed from your hand, who now maligns you so?

[*Seguwa has fled at sight of Edufa*]

Chorus: We implore you, tell us she lies. We do not believe her, pious one. Tell us she lies.

Senchi: Friends, what is this?

Edufa: [*Dejectedly on the steps*] If you see my father, call him back that I may weep on his shoulder.

Chorus: Great God, is it true that she is dead?

Senchi: [*Shaking him*] Edufa. Friend. What's all this about charms?

Edufa: [*Violent, his voice unnatural*] I burned it.

[*He slouches helplessly on the steps*]

Senchi: Stand up, man. What in the name of mystery is it all about?

Chorus One: Do you hear him? He buried it, he says. There was something then? Edufa, is it true what this woman says? That Ampoma is dead, and in your place?

Edufa:	…and buried… [*Wildly*] I told her not to swear. I did not know that harm could be done. I did not know it. [*Looking belligerently at Senchi, and not recognizing him*] Who are you? Why are you looking at me?
Senchi:	[*Sadly*] Senchi.
Chorus One:	He is raving.
Edufa:	I told her not to swear. I didn't know that harm could be done.
Chorus:	Not to swear, or harm could be done. Alas!
Senchi:	[*Seizing hold of him*] Tell me all, Edufa.

[*The owl hoots outside*]

Edufa:	[*Wildly*] Didn't he take that bird away? [*He looks at Senchi dangerously*] who are you? Don't restrain me. [*Straining with more than natural strength*] Where is my club? Where is my leopard skin? I'll teach death to steal my wives. [*So strong that Senchi can no longer restrain him*] Death I will lie closely at the grave again, I'll grab you, unlock her from your grip and bring her safely home to my bed. And until then, no woman's hand shall touch me.
Chorus:	She is dead. [*They rush into Edufa's rooms*]
Senchi:	[*With infinite sadness*] There, Edufa, there… don't rave so. No… not this. [*He attempts to hold him again*]
Edufa:	[*Wrenching himself free*] The last laugh will be mine when I bring her home again. I will bring Ampoma back. Forward to the grave. [*He moves in strength towards the back courtyard roaring*] I will do it ! … I am conqueror..? [*His last word, however, comes as a great questioning lament*] Conqueror?

[*The Chorus returns mournfully. Senchi makes his way past them into Edufa's rooms*]

Chorus: [*Several voices together, and a single voice every now and then, as they make their way out through the gate; rendered at a slow dirge tempo*]
Calamity.
That we should be the witnesses.
Do not restrain your tears,
Let them stream,
Make a river of sorrow, for Ampoma is dead.
We do not know how,
We do not understand,
But she is dead.
Will someone go and tell mother!
Edufa! Edufa!
How is it possible
That she is dead?

[*They can be heard beating their clappers and chanting. Senchi returns. He stands, alone on the steps*]

Senchi: Blank. I have ended up blank once again. All that is left, the laughter of the flowers in her lifeless arms, and the lingering smell of incense. [*He descends*]
And over me, the taut extension of the sky — to which I raise my song.
Will someone go and tell her mother?
[*He sings*]: And if I find you
I'll have worship you
I must adore you
Nne
Nne nne
O mother
Nne
Nne me

Sorrowfully
(p) O___ child of A - ma, child of A-ma in___ the
night Is___ wan-der-ing, Cry-ing, Mm-m-m, ___
How my moth-er is pon - der-ing.
O, child of A - ma Why is she wan - der-ing, ___
Why wan - der-ing, Why wan-d'ring in the night
Like the dy - ing?___ Me - wuo!___
Our moth-er's dead, Ei! Ei - Ei!
We the or-phans cry, Our moth-er's dead,
O! O - O! We the or-phans cry.

Alla marcia
(f) Gen - tle-men, show me___ a thought you've
thought through, and I'll bow to you right low and_
grant you a mas-ter's due. Fea - ther-fine
la - dies with hips that rhyme,
who the blaz-es minds your child-ren's man-ners at this
time? Left, right, left, does__ not
feed a na-tion. I'd ra-ther have you
roar-ing drunk at a harv-est ce - le - bra-tion.

Alla marcia
(f) Gen - tle-men, show me a thought you've
thought through, and I'll bow to you right low and
grant you a mas-ter's due. Fea - ther-fine
la - dies with hips that rhyme,
who the blaz-es minds your child-ren's man-ners at this
time? Left, right, left, does not
feed a na-tion. I'd ra-ther have you
roar-ing drunk at a harv-est ce - le - bra-tion.